WIS

REIKI

IN EVERYDAY LIVING

*How Universal Energy Is
A Natural Part of
Life, Medicine, and Personal Growth.*

Earlene F. Gleisner, RN/RM

White Feather Press
Laytonville, California

REIKI IN EVERYDAY LIVING
*How Universal Energy is a Natural Part
of Life, Medicine, and Personal Growth*

by: Earlene Gleisner, RN/RM

Published by: White Feather Press
POB 1209
Laytonville, CA 95454

**All rights reserved. No part of this book may
be translated, reproduced or transmitted in
any form or by any means, electronic or mecha-
nical, including photocopying, recording, or
by any information storage and retrieval
system without written permission from the
author, except for the inclusion of brief
quotations in a review.**

Copyright c 1992 by Earlene F. Gleisner
First Printing - August, 1992
Second Printing - October, 1993
Printed in the United State of America

**Reference and Quotes of The Twelve Pathways
are reprinted from Handbook to Higher
Consciousness by Ken Keyes, Jr, Fifth edition,
Copyright 1975 by the Living Love Center.**

Publishers cataloging in Publication Data
Gleisner, Earlene F.
REIKI in Everyday Living: How Universal Energy
is a Natural Part of Life, Medicine, and Personal Growth.
1. Title   2. Holistic Health
3. Healing, Self-healing

Library of Congress
 Catalog Card Number 92-97021
ISBN 1-880357-07-0 $12.95 PB/Softcover

This Book is Dedicated to ....

Those of us

who are willing

to touch ourselves

and each other

with love and

with caring hands

October, 1991
Laytonville, CA

REIKI IN EVERYDAY LIVING

Table of Contents

Acknowledgements

My specific thanks go to my husband, Yuwach, and my friend and fellow REIKI Master, Victoria Suzanne Crane. They have stood by me when thoughts ran smoothly onto the page and during the long, frustrating days when thoughts and words were scattered in different directions. I thank the many who read the essay drafts and gave comment, especially Linda Boutiette, Kathy Reynolds, Marian Franklin, Margaret Fetty, John Crane, Liz Arkley-Warren, Joanne Wilkes, and Chris Barbano, and Joanie Mitchell.

I also honor and acknowledge every student who has shared themselves in class, all who dare to ask for more in life and from living, and the many who bless themselves daily by struggling through the process of self-realization and who are learning the art of "being." I especially honor anyone who asks how they may be a part of their own healing and that of our Earth.

"RAKEY"

One afternoon in 1977, while driving on the outskirts of a farming community through freshly-turned fields of earth, my then seven-year-old daughter looked at the regular furrows and called out "Rakey." She said she thought that God had pulled a huge rake through the soil, making "big dents." When I looked where her eyes were pointing, I saw shimmering heat dance near undulating ground within slanted sunlight and I thrilled with the sense of earth's vitality and potential growth. Now that I know the term REIKI as a name for Universal Life Energy in the Usui System of Natural Healing, I continue to hold that spectacle of shimmering vibration as my tangible picture of this energy.

At the time of my daughter's announcement, I was working as a Registered Nurse in a hospital and growing disillusioned with the bright light/cold steel approach to cures. Rebelling against dehumanizing procedures and treatments, I began my search for more wholeness in health and healing.

In 1984, after many classes and much reading, as well as innumerable life and lifestyle changes and a Vision Quest, I found REIKI, or rather, REIKI found me.

Since then, time and experience has deepened and lengthened my understanding of this energy and, because I continue to work at a Rural Health Clinic in various capacities, I am finding more and more methods of application.

A primary theme of this collection of essays and poems is to demystify REIKI so that its effectiveness as a system and as an energy can be documented and accepted as complementary to all systems of health care. A secondary theme is to illustrate how I believe REIKI, when used in everyday living, can increase the quality of life.

Realizing there will never be enough words to discuss all there is to know and experience about REIKI, and knowing there are so many ways to connect and reconnect with whatever name you use to behold, "life energy," I acknowledge that all the words written here are from my point of view and developed from my own experience.

My hope is that this book also will provide all students and potential students of REIKI with added tools and methods of application. I hope it will increase your excitement over the promise you hold in your hands, and will encourage you to use this precious gift with responsibility and respect.

Love and Tantay (Peace),

Darlene

What REIKI Is!

It may seem that REIKI is an intangible, an impossibility in your hand. Something beyond your grasp.

Take heart! What you have experienced in First Degree class has been both an opening and a healing. REIKI is already working in you, on your life and on everything you are touching.

Because each of us is different, I try to minimize, in classes, any attention paid to "hot hands." The focus on this singular type of sensation can be an impediment to your trust. Too often conversation between students becomes a comparison of how hot or cold each others hands are.

Your impression of how REIKI comes through you cannot be compared to another's. Your experience is uniquely your own. Just as unique is your sense of REIKI being transferred to another. There is no place here for competition, because REIKI is not in competition with anything or anybody. REIKI just IS. You may feel, see, or sense it as warmth or coolness, light or bright, vibrations or bubbles. Whatever the sensation, the only importance this feeling has is that **when** it changes or shifts its expression, **then** is the time to move your hands to their next position. Whatever sensation you perceive in your hand or your mind is merely a manifestation of your unique presence in your world as you relate to it.

Once you've opened to REIKI, you'll never lose it. Some students admit they don't practice REIKI on others or their own bodies, and, after a while, talk themselves into believing that it has gone away. REIKI, however, is forever flowing. The only thing these students have not been practicing is their attention. They have become unconscious of its flow. Be assured that throughout each day and each night, whenever a need for energy is touched, REIKI will be channeled.

Think now! What is the first instinctive move made when someone is seen in either emotional or physical pain? When a child has pinched a finger or bumped a knee? When an animal is ill? When a tree is broken? What do we do for ourselves when we have an upset stomach or a leg cramp? We reach out and touch the person, our child, an animal, the tree, ourselves.

REIKI is at hand in each of these moments, pulsating toward the need that started it drawing through the vessel of our bodies. REIKI balances and energizes everything in its path, even you and I as it flows through each of us.

REIKI brings about change.

These changes are unpredictable and limitless. Thus it is useless for us to set up any kind of expectation around these changes. The healings created may be entirely different than what you or I would expect. We really cannot know what would be best for each other's personhood or our own well-being.

REIKI facilitates changes which are the most appropriate for each of us because it energizes and balances **our** systems as **we each** have uniquely created them.

If we can release our judgement and expectation and let go, and if we can flow with the balancing and re-energizing changes that occur in our body while reviewing any insight or awareness that comes up in our minds, REIKI will work wonders on all levels. Damaging patterns of behavior can be recognized and cleared or, at least, more awareness of them can result.

For instance, when I began using REIKI, I became aware that I had a habit of putting people in categories and diagnosing their problems in a very clinical fashion. With REIKI, I was no longer able to remain unattached and this barrier to more intimate friendships was reduced.

REIKI helps clients on whom we work become more aware of themselves in new ways. For example, one man who had experienced a painful knee for 13 years had to ask himself why he missed the pain when it disappeared after one full-body session.

Not all clients will be comfortable with this or any new awareness. Some will praise the sense of relaxation and energy directly after a session but discount the entire experience the next day. Others will receive an awareness about diet or relationship problems while on the table, but lose faith in the suggestions when they are called upon to take action. Many will cry or laugh or holler spontaneously. A few will sit up in the middle of the session and say they want to leave.

No matter what occurs, it is best to stand in a place of allowing, for, in this place, there is no expectation and there is no judgement. Here, within each of us, REIKI flows.

For those who will come with their questions, fears, and skepticism, we can ask them to sit or recline comfortably while we gently place our hands on them in the precise manner of the Usui System of Natural Healing. We can ask them to breathe deeply, and release their tension while focusing on the pressure of our hands on their body or on any sensations they may feel in the area under our hands, and/or any sensation in their body.

We might ask them if they feel anything un-usual. If they cannot answer, we don't have to try to explain to them what it is they should be feeling. We must let them be. REIKI will create an answer for them in their own experience. We may never know what that is.

It's not up to you or to me to pontificate or recruit anyone into believing in something to which they cannot relate. We are not a religious cult or a movement or an organization that demands all its members believe a certain way.

We are only humans searching to make our world and lives more meaningful, with a little less tension. Friends or clients may prefer massage or Tai Chi, or Karate, or any of the other innumerable ways available to help us understand ourselves and this world.

REIKI may not be for everyone, and yet................

REIKI will be working in the most surprising ways. We can only show up so as to live our own lives and touch what comes before us.

Very Personally Yours

The only commitment I ask of First Degree students is that they work on themselves and their own healing. This is part of my growing belief that to increase the positiveness of life and have any possibility of creating change for our world, we each must take responsibility for ourselves.

In the beginning of my time with REIKI, I forgot these very teachings of TAKATA:

First, heal yourself

Then, your family and friends,

Only then work on others

I came away from my First Degree class ready and willing to heal the world. I offered my hands everywhere until I began to worry: "Why weren't my hands feeling the same as when I had finished the class?" and "Why was I having difficulty focusing on others in a nurturing way?" I became short-tempered with mood swings and very, very tired.

I found myself wondering if REIKI really was the method I had been seeking. I remained concerned until I re-experienced another First Degree class and realized that every time I did a REIKI session, I was bringing the energy through my body and was being treated first.

It is the same for everyone.

Universal Life Energy pours through our bodies, filling **our** needs **before** it transfers to another person's need. This allows us to remain at an even level of energy during multiple sessions for others. **It also means that when we have a more-than-average imbalance in ourselves, physically, mentally, or emotionally, we use REIKI at the same or at a greater rate than our capacity to channel it.**

It became extremely important then for me to focus on my own needs and attitudes so I could return to the "allowing" mode. I realized I would be unable to be present for another in my best, non-judgmental way if I was so depleted I couldn't work on my own issues.

Takata's words resonated in my head:

First, Heal yourself

Thus, self-treatment has become my most important tool.

This can be accomplished by following the same precise system learned in class.

What follows here is an abbreviated outline describing Personal Hand Positions:

HEAD - First Position:

The palms of your hand butt against your cheek bone and your fingers lay a-cross your eyes and your frontal sinuses (forehead). Elbows can be supported on the arms of a chair or pillows if you're sitting up or laying down. You might want to put a pillow between your arms if you're laying on your side.

HEAD - Second Position:

The edges of your palms are placed over your ears with fingers pressing the area just over your temples.

HEAD - Third Position:

Your hands can be layered across the back of your head rather than going from the occipital ridge (back of head where nerves from spine enter into the base of the

HEAD - Fourth Position (Thyroid):

Place your hands on top of each other at base of your throat.

HEAD - Fifth Position (Thymus):

Place your hands on top of each other on your sternum (breast bone.)

Optional Positions:

Your hands can be placed over your ears or under your chin or across your jaw line.

FRONT:

All positions on the trunk of your body can be reached by placing your right hand on your right side and your left hand on your left side. Starting as high as you want or need, continue down until you can no longer reach comfortably while reclining.

Your knees and feet are more easily done sitting so you can bring one foot then the other toward you. If this is not possible, the act of applying hands to your inguinal or groin area will be effective.

BACK:

Your neck and shoulders can be reached while sitting in a chair or reclining and a more comfortable position accomplished with pillows supporting your arms while sitting or while lying down.

Your back receives REIKI as your hands travel down the front of your trunk because REIKI transfers from one cell to the next, once the need in the first cell has been met. Thus you treat your front and your back at the same time.

To enhance this process, visualize the 'allowing' of REIKI through your body to the edge of the skin on your back where it touches the material of the bed. Breathe slowly and evenly.

*   *   *   *

Treating yourself is sometimes hampered by the fact that you may not get clear-cut messages from your hands in areas of need. Shifts in sensations are less easily noticed so you can just move your hands when the hand-position becomes tiring. Remember to use breath to assist your relaxation.

Of course, REIKI is always at hand for small

accidents during the day and when you feel depleted of energy. If you notice early symptoms of a cold, place one hand on the Thymus position while steering the car with the other. This can help to boost your immune system.

Be aware that your body is sending you a message at this time and needs rest and more complete attention.

In the tapes and stories we have found of Takata, we know that she treated herself every morning. She acknowledged herself and brought her energies into balance so that she could live her day in fullness. She lived her own words.

I'm asking you to accept REIKI as an integral part of your life too, and make it very personally yours.

REIKI and Personal Clarity

Using REIKI on a daily basis can help provide wellness. It is a way in which we can acknowledge our own needs in a healthy way and support our physical well-being. Giving ourselves regular REIKI also acknowledges our personal responsibility for that well-being.

Becoming aware of a general need for the balancing energy of REIKI is not limited to the physical plane. Granted, our physical symptoms are generally the ones to which we pay more close attention. Our physical needs, however, are often dictated by mental, emotional and spiritual ones.

A small burn at the stove or a cut finger or a bumped head are all times when we need a "quick hit of soothing REIKI."

The moment these needs occur, I now am

learning to stop what I am doing, because I believe something within me has brought my body to this point of injury. I have taught myself to settle into the moment, REIKI my injury, take a deep breath, and ask myself, "OK, what's going on here?"

I usually find that I have been or have become distracted by trying to solve too many issues at one time or by trying to bring more than one project to a successful conclusion. I find that I am worried, or angry, or scattered and not truly focusing on the world around me. Consequently, the world I've bumped into is calling for my attention by helping me to create my personal injury. It's reminding me to "Be Here Now!"

Placing my hand on my injury is an opportunity to assess the situation, reprioritize, reaffirm my commitment to living richly, and resettle into my center.

Sometimes, in that moment, I realize I need to ask for help or to admit to myself I've created a negative attitude. I may simply need 'time out' and can do this by looking through a window or at a favorite corner in my home or having a good laugh at the situation or even a good cry.

Many personal crises express themselves in these small physical injuries, and some are expressed as larger ones. Others may occur in the form of a disease and can range in severity from an acute cold to a chronic illness or specific areas of disease such as tumors.

Concern has been expressed frequently in classes about doing REIKI over these tumors. "Won't the energy cause them to grow bigger?" The answer is that REIKI will assist the body to do what it needs to do to heal itself. You and I cannot know what that will be. In some cases, the tumor does grow larger until it collapses. In other cases, the tumor shrinks. Still in others, there is no physical change at all, but the individual finds increased peace. In a few, the ultimate healing of death arrives quicker.

We must remember in all these cases that REIKI does not nurture illness. REIKI strengthens healthy tissue as well as all body defenses. REIKI brings about balance and embraces each individual's wellness as it needs to be expressed.

REIKI helps each of us begin to listen to our inner voice that is crying out for attention. While using our REIKI hands to strengthen our bodies, we can take time to relax, rest, dream, reassess and reaffirm our beingness. Remember, it is often true: the longer a condition has existed, the longer the time needed for any of us to relinquish it.

Other personal crises are "in the middle of the nighters"! Wakefulness, while meaning anything, can be distressful. Issues abound, for me, at 4AM. In fact, I think someone is awake somewhere at all different times of the night keeping vigil over the frets, frustrations, and issues of the human condition.

As I have watched thoughts and concerns cross my mind in this personal darkness, I have begun to notice different areas of my body experiencing different tensions. I have discovered if I place my hands over the tensed part of my body and breathe as evenly as possible, I can begin to attain relaxation and eventually return to sleep. Sometimes my REIKI hands chase discomfort all over my body for the rest of the night. I either breathe and continue to move my hands from place to place or I do a complete, systematic session. If the distress doesn't go away, I have been known to get up and do journal writing or make lists. Usually, however, I am able to fall back to sleep with my hands in place on some receding strain.

This experience of noting different degrees of tension in different parts of my body has been transformational. I have come to recognize how certain issues cause distinguishably different tensions in different parts of my body.

I also have begun to recognize these sensations during the light of day as a response to all kinds of daily situations. Confrontations, family squabbles or community conflicts bring these about, as well as, emotions or emotional questions, personal insights, or developing spiritual awareness. When these occur, I place my hands on the tense or painful part of my body, and I, literally, hang on.

If I'm in public, this usually assists me in remaining calm while addressing the crisis at hand.

When I'm alone, I am using a technique I've developed to assist me in gaining clarity regarding myself or the situation while letting REIKI nurture my body part. This helps me come to know on a deeper level what is going on. I am calling this technique:

PERSONAL ASSESSMENT PROCESS

One: I Recognize

In this stage, it is enough if I only become aware of the part of my body that is in tension or in pain and I place my hands there. I am noticing and accepting the message my body is giving me. This can be anything from a sudden dry or sore throat to a cold, headache, a shuddering feeling in an area above my navel and/or an open-hole feeling at the base of my stomach.

Two: I Reveal

Because I accept the belief that emotions can get stuck in cells of the body, I reveal the name the emotion that is expressing itself as tension or pain as quickly as possible without judgement.

At one time, a sudden dry throat would always occur just as I was going to speak up on an issue. I discovered when I held the area and quickly named the emotion, it was "Fear." This non-judgmental acknowledgment of emotion has led to a finer discernment of fear, such as fear of failure, fear of success, fear of recognition, fear of challenge. While I am applying REIKI and declaring my emotion, I can tell when I'm in tune with my inner voice because my body will relax with a deep breath.

If I haven't stated the most accurate emotion, I do not experience this relaxing breath. I then encourage myself to try again.

Three: I Explore

Whatever feeling or emotion I have identified in a specific part of my body can have bonded memories that are reinforcing its presence.

These memories are usually from childhood and/or maturing experiences. This is called imprinting. Thus while holding the part of my body which is in tension, I invite a picture to present itself. I begin by looking at what just happened in my immediate present to cause this tension. I then explore my own role and those of others in the present incident. Breathing slowly so that I can remain relaxed, I ask for any corresponding memory from my past.

This step takes trust and practice. It can bring immense understanding of how I repeat lessons until I learn them. It can also illustrate erroneous perceptions from my childhood or help me define an outgrown coping pattern or some left-over emotions from unresolved issues.

Four: I Release

Believing in the theory that recognizing patterns in life and relationships is one important step in making changes, I now bless these moments of clarity. In this way, I am releasing the hold that I feel previous experiences have had on my present life situations.

Breathing slowly again while still holding with my REIKI hands, I feel the pressure/pain reduce. If I have correctly Recognized, Revealed, and Explored the pain, it is Released and replaced by the warmth and fullness of REIKI.

These four steps have become a tremendous help in my coping with the challenges and confrontations in my life. They have assisted me in knowing myself and in growing to be more available to others while still being honest with who I am.

I acknowledge that this is of course not the only way. There are many, many more methods of personal work that can be complemented with REIKI hands. Whatever our inclination or interest, whichever method or personal process we may choose, we can nurture our self-hood, our very being, with REIKI as we work toward greater personal clarity.

Our bodies are the manifestation of our spirit for here and now. It is what we have to work with so that we each can get around and live our lives. Our bodies give us messages regarding our total needs and well-being. We can learn to honor these messages so as to keep our human overcoats healthy so that each will serve in total balance when we step forward to care for another.

Gifts For The Giver

Any REIKI Master can show an individual how to accomplish a total body session and can facilitate an opening and connection with REIKI, but until each individual personally feels his/her own exceptional sense of this energy, there can be difficulty in accepting this process as real.

Any friend or teacher can also point out, suggest, or explain whatever they suppose is our talent or 'specialness'. Inner acceptance of who we each are is what finally helps to develop that inner knowing of our unique talent or 'specialness' in life and gives us that undeniable sense of self.

Standing in our center and allowing REIKI to flow through us, getting out of the way of expectation and trusting in the message of our hands are all ways of attaining personal growth and spiritual enhancement. It is also the way of coming to terms with our 'self' and obtaining inner acceptance.

There is no need for our mind to do anything during a session. Our "being-ness" is enough. This is a form of inner acceptance, of stretching to the very edge of who we are in one small moment and allowing in our hearts and head that this moment is all there is.

Consistent use of REIKI on ourselves and/or others (be that 'other' a tree or an animal or another person) is one way in which to become attuned to who and what we are and to help us become "aware" of other things about ourselves.

As we quietly 'do' REIKI, we slow ourselves down and become more cognizant of feelings, odors, color, taste. We can more clearly perceive our physical, mental, and emotional relationships. With this understanding and acceptance, we begin to recognize projects, events, and actions and discover in ourselves a skill, flair, or knowingness that we may have been only marginally aware of previously or that was totally non-evident to us. This, then, becomes the genius of ourselves that Takata said REIKI would bring out in each of us, whatever that genius is.

Now, many of us try to choose the gift or genius that is ours. In this New Age, channeling an alien entity and documenting wisdom-filled words in a book might be an aspect you would greatly desire. Or, perhaps, you would like to paint pictures or create inspired stained-glass windows.

These gifts or talents are not impossible. However, the act of saying, "This is what I want to do," may limit your possibilities by focusing on one desired potential.

Learning to release expectation and open ourselves to all the possibilities of life will, then, assist us in becoming aware of those exceptional qualities that are ours.

Perhaps we have the skill to listen to another person, or to design a better wheelchair. We may be able to paint a wall, grow seed into vegetables, detect a change in weather by our sense of smell, empathize with a friend. The list of possibilities are endless and becoming aware of more than one gift or genius is made possible by accepting the one that comes to us first.

When we acknowledge that which we do well, we ultimately accept our gift or genius and use it for the benefit of ourselves and everyone around us. Chances are, as we grow in the awareness of ourself as a REIKI channel, we will more easily accept ourself and our individuality. Then, our capacity of self-awareness will increase and we will see what else there is for us in our lives. That which we may have desired to do may then be actualized with greater ease and deeper insight than originally envisioned.

CHANGES

In the quiet practice of REIKI

    on plant or animal or self

Spiritual growth increases

    inner knowing develops

And our connection

    with all things,

        grows,

Intensifying a hundred - fold

    by the act

    of our touching

    another.

1990

Reflections

The very idea that I, as a practitioner of REIKI, would be stimulating my personal and spiritual growth by simply 'doing' a session on myself or another, has intrigued me from the moment I read the advertisement claim in Common Ground in 1983.

In the brochure I received from Rev. Fran Brown, who I eventually chose as my teacher, I was promised, "REIKI is an impetus to spiritual growth." Although I wasn't born in the "show me" state, I did want to know how and why.

After a few months of practicing REIKI, I began to experience an openness to new understandings of myself and of my circumstances. It was as if I were viewing life around me differently, as if the window panes of my perception had been washed or I was able to look at myself through different windows. REIKI was focusing my attention in a new way on myself and my relationships.

I began to develop a sense of belonging, but not to a social group or to an organization. "To what then?" I had to ask myself. The belonging, I'm beginning to believe, was and is to myself and to all that is.

I've pondered the change and talked to many others who "do" REIKI. We agree that some kind of personal growth work occurs and there is an expansion within our "self" and consciousness while we are practicing REIKI regularly.

That is the "key": practicing REIKI regularly. This can be on our body, our cat or our favorite animal, a tree, or on another human being.

The very idea of allowing our bodies to be a vehicle by which this energy, REIKI, transfers from the Universe to another is an experience in letting go, of standing in our centers and "being". At the same time you and I are letting go, we need to be totally present so that as practitioners we may be aware of our hands and have the experience of feeling the shift in the energy when an area is filled. Because we sense this shift, we know when to move onto the next area of the body we are working on.

When I read any of the several books on enlightenment, "letting go" and "living in the present" are the first essential attitudes mandated.

In the 'Handbook to Higher Consciousness - The Science of Happiness' by Ken Keyes, the first three of his Twelve Pathways are categorized under "Freeing Myself" and the second three are grouped under "Being Here Now."

In 'Grist for the Mill', Ram Dass translates "NAMASTE", a greeting, to mean: "I honor the place in you where the entire universe resides. I honor the place in you of love, of light, of truth, of peace. I honor the place within you where if you are in that place in you and I am in that place in me, there is only one of us." He continues a little farther in the book; "So that the next time you sit waiting for something to begin you will realize there is nothing that needs to begin, for the beginning, the middle, and the end are already who you are."

When we place our hands on another person in the practice of REIKI, we are actualizing that 'being-ness'; we are standing in the beginning, the middle, and the end. We are freeing ourselves from the tentacles of thought and judgement and settling into our central core. We are joining and becoming one with whatever and whomever we are touching. We are living in the moment, and there is truly "only one of us."

The third category in Ken Keyes' book is "Interacting with Others." Laying hands on another person's clothed or unclothed body is an interaction. When interaction can be done without expectation, it becomes unconditional love. This act can release us from the illusion of separateness that often clouds our minds. The act of laying hands on a tree, a plant, an animal, or any living thing can also support that release and bring us to a new level of openness.

Reading our hands and coming to know when there is a change so we can recognize when to move to the next position becomes a lesson in trusting our inner voice. The fact that we DO move our hands is an experience in taking action based on information from that same voice or inner knowingness. This accomplishes the fourth category of the Twelve Pathways, "Discovering My Conscious Awareness," which states in the 10th path:

> "I am continually calming the restless scanning of my rational mind in order to perceive the finer energies that enable me to unitively merge with everything around me."

We are perceiving the finer energies of REIKI and "merging with everything" during a session.

It is amazing to understand that the very simple act of performing a REIKI session is intrinsically tied into the lessons of spiritual growth:

* releasing the events of life and allowing the sensation of REIKI to flow through body, mind, and spirit;

*   being conscious of the 'here and now'

*   coming into interaction with another through the laying-on-of-hands without expectation but purely out of love

*   listening and trusting and taking action on any awareness that occurs during a session.

Simply put, the practice of REIKI is a catalyst for expanding our awareness of ourselves, our work, and our spiritual growth while making stronger our connection with all that is.

SPIRITUAL PRECEPTS OF REIKI

Just for Today...

Do Not Anger

Just for Today...

Do not Worry

Honor your parents,

teachers, and elders

Earn your living honestly

Show gratitude to all

living beings.

The Precepts

In the beginning of my experience with REIKI, I had a grudging belief that attention to the Precepts would be of assistance to me.

The origins of the Precepts continue to be clouded by the creativity of our oral-history tradition. Wording is shaded differently by each Master who teaches. I now have seen and heard the Precepts presented in many different ways and have come to understand that it is in the original wording by Takata that these guides retain their most value. Viewed in the context of her phrasing, they represent attitudes toward life.

On a taped recording of a class given before she made her transition, Hawayo Takata, Grand Master of REIKI from 1940 to 1980, listed the Precepts in the following manner:

1. Just for Today, Do Not Anger

2. Just for Today, Do Not Worry

3. We must count our blessings and honor our fathers and mothers, and our teachers and neighbors and honor our food by making no waste and show gratitude for all this also.

4. Make your living honestly

5. Be kind to everything that has life.

REIKI Master Victoria Suzanne Crane has extensively investigated the origins of REIKI and has found them intrinsically bound to Buddhist teachings. She has detailed the correspondence of these REIKI Precepts as antidotes for the Five Hindrances to all growth as detailed by Buddha in his teaching at Deer Pond. When I look at these Precepts in this light, I can see more clearly how they can affect my life and learning.

As a wife and mother, worry was the first Precept I began to work on. Worry was a habit for me, I discovered, as it seems to be for most of society.

Pick a subject! Any subject! I bet that either you or I can find at least one detail in that subject that can act as a source for worry. Have you ever given attention to what happens in your body or in your life when you begin to worry about something in the past, present, or future?

Try this. For just a moment, focus on one of your worry items and pay attention to how your body feels.

Mine feels as if all the cells have huddled together, clinging to each other, allowing no space between them. I feel closed in on myself, unable to see into the world around me. The words "Threat" and "Fear" enter my brain and twist around and through my consciousness leaving no room for other thoughts, let alone other possibilities.

Worry has pushed everything else out of the way and has closed me off from the outside. The act of worrying has the side effect of closing me off from the source of REIKI and shutting me down as a channel.

If worry is the internalization of Fear, then Anger is the externalization of it.

Now choose a topic of anger and feel your body again.

Mine feels as if all the cells have been dammed up and are reservoirs of blood and held breaths and screams. My cells feel engorged and pushed so close together, there is no space between them. I feel tight inside and every part of me is shaking with tension.

Again, I feel stuck, shut down. Only when I

choose to relinquish the total involvement with either of these emotions do I feel my breath flow in and out and do I begin to realize again my openness to REIKI and to life.

In a story about anger, Takata shared her learning experience about this Precept with several of her students. She had become a Master and Dr. Hayashi was traveling with her and helping her create and teach classes throughout Hawaii. On the boat trip from Japan, her cabin mate had been in need of money and Takata had cheerfully helped her. This woman, however, had continued to return again and again for more help, making promises to return the money she had borrowed and then breaking her promises. Takata admitted she was becoming furious but, because she was trying to live by the Precepts, she continued to recount the good points of this woman and to assist her without anger.

At her wits end, she finally told Dr. Hayashi, admitted her anger, and asked what she could do about the situation.

Dr. Hayashi apparently shook his head at her and said, "The Precepts only say, Do Not Anger. They do NOT say never to DO anything about it."

Later when Takata saw the woman in question, walking toward her house, she met her on the porch. Before the woman could speak, Takata pointed to the steps of the porch, "See those steps?" she asked. "They go both ways. Please go down them and never come back!"

These two statement Do Not Anger and Do Not Worry, are not asking us to stuff our emotions or to push them away so as not to acknowledge them. These Precepts of REIKI invite us to look at those emotions and investigate the sources of their hold on us and thread our way toward the realization of their origins. In this way we may be able to acknowledge their presence and do something about them before they constrict our lives.

When I discovered that worry and anger were versions of fear, I began a dialogue with myself about my personal fears by asking myself to look at what was the worst possible thing that could happen to me around any feared situation. Once I have developed an answer, I then ask myself if there is any action I can take to move away from this outcome, or if I can live with this possibility.

I am allowing this feeling of fear to become a "sign post" which simply tells me to review a situation. I am more able to feel and deal with my emotions, and ultimately relinquish them by logically dealing with the various situations that have inspired the feelings. I find I am relieved of the burden of constantly worrying about an event or a circumstance or of becoming angry at it. I feel I have learned how to "get out of the way" of the situations of my life and move on.

I am more able to move past each crisis with fewer incapacitating moments of emotion and with more honest sensations of feeling. For the most part, anger and fear are no longer constricting my life or my attention or, more importantly, the flow of REIKI.

The third Precept has many component parts when taken the way Takata last stated them. Honoring those who teach us, not only our parents, but all teachers, can bring honor to ourselves. It can strengthen our ties to our origins and give us some concept of where we've come from. When we also honor those who are part of our lineage as REIKI practitioners, we can then strengthen our tie to the passage of this energy.

Honoring our food is more than being grateful for the bounty of our lives. What we choose to feed our minds, our bodies, and our spirits is a statement of how we wish to grow and how we honor ourselves.

Making no waste is asking that we know how much we need to use, how much we are willing to share, and how well we are taking care of what we have. There is no waste when we also compost and recycle. All is used and honored and makes great sense in this day and age of hunger, homelessness, and contamination.

"Show gratitude for all this also" refers not just to food and teachers, but to all experiences, blessings, and opportunities that make up our lives.

When I forget to show gratitude or acknowledge compliments or a rewarding experience, etc., I lose track of them and they are not sealed into my consciousness. If I do that often enough, I find I lose a sense of the bounty of my life and tend to get a little depressed.

Counting my blessings then becomes a way to turn my attention around to a more positive frame of reference. Consciously showing gratitude seems to bring more things to mind for which to be grateful. It teaches me to allow myself to receive and affirms my connection with the abundance of the Universe. Separateness disappears and I feel at one with all things.

The next Precept of "Make Your Living Honestly" speaks on two levels: (1) Making the effort to earn a living, and (2) Doing it in a fashion which acknowledges abundance and potential.

Creating a business, digging a ditch, painting a picture, for instance, are each efforts by individuals to establish a focus for personal expression. This action helps to create a bond with life and opens a pathway to receivership so that the honor of payment is also created. This may be in the form of money, bartered goods, or self-reward. This is also showing personal responsibility for taking care of one's self and one's needs.

When we can accomplish our livelihood to the best of our ability and with honesty, we can be open and more able to attract honesty in others and draw prosperity to ourselves.

Thus, not creating a job or not doing it honestly creates feelings of deprivation and desperation. These feelings can often lead to such negative actions as theft and lies. These negativisms can close down our channel.

The final Precept, "Being Kind to Every Living Thing," reminds me that I am not alone, that I am a part of the whole of the living universe, and that I am not above or below anything or anyone else. This reminds me that we are all equal and puts me in touch with the living essence of energy that flows through all beings and things, be it a tree or a flower or an animal. Even the elements of the earth that have become chemicals and form plastics or rugs have energy. I am more able to understand the philosophy of the American Indian, "All that casts a shadow has spirit."

When I read these Precepts to a new class, I read them more slowly now. I am finding that they embody an element of reason and reassurance in their wording that helps me remember I can do no more than live this day. The flow of words suggests I always have another chance. If I lose my conscious intent and become angry or worried or wasteful or if I forget that I am a part of all that is, I will always have the opportunity to try again.

Because these five statements are more like guides or suggestions, the responsibility for incorporating them into our lives rests solely within each of us. We are gently asked to become our own center with the Precepts of REIKI acting as the next steps to our spiritual growth, to our emotional maturity, mental clarity, and ultimately, to our total well-being.

DIFFERENT DECISIONS

What do others do
   When there's no one there to love?
   Do they run with freedom
              or with fear?
   Do they cry or laugh?
   Play solitaire?
         My heart hardens a little!

What do others do
   When there's no place, anywhere
              for peace?
   Do they stride with steady pace
         through their lives?
                  Or stumble?
   Do they scream?
   Or adjust?
         My soul dies a little!

What do other do
   When there's no person
              to give them love?
   Do they run from another to
              another?
   Reaching at all who turn away?
   Do they touch more and feel less?
   Or walk in the sun alone?
         I eat too much!

1976

A Lifetime Of Decisions

This experience we call life is filled to the brim with decisions. During every waking moment, we are faced with more choices than we can possibly comprehend.

We are often semi- or un-conscious of the threads of life we spin with each thought or direction of thought our minds take. Some decisions are merely reactionary; some are carefully and methodically made. Some major resolutions are brought about by a culmination of seemingly inconsequential decisions and most have small conclusions intertwined in their process.

One growing realization of mine stands out here: my decisions today are affected greatly by the choices I made yesterday.

As an example, to be able to decide what to have for dinner, I must take into consideration what I decided to buy at the store. I had to choose a day to go shopping in the first place. I also had to consider what my family would eat based on recipe-searching and preparation and individual likes and dislikes of each one of them, plus my knowledge of who is on a special diet and what all of our schedules are for the day. Adding further to the background of the choice, while shopping, I had to have figured out how much money I had to spend and, initially, choose a method of earning money so I could spend it.

The point I'm trying to make here is that I have brought to this particular decision, as I do to every one of my decisions, the entirety of my past experience. I have brought my understanding of who I am and what I can accomplish in a given period of time, my known likes and dislikes as of this moment, my understanding of those I live with, and my projection of who I am or want to be in the future along with what my goals are for today, next year, and so forth.

All that we are and have experienced is embodied in every single decision we make and each decision creates a new experience. Until we make any decision, we have no real idea of what the experience will be. Thus, we never really make mistakes; we only create experiences we either like or dislike.

The only difficult part of this concept is agreeing to the facts that (1) each of us is really free to make any choice we want and (2) we can create change by choosing to do so.

As a teen-ager I decided to believe that smoking cigarettes looked grown-up and that I liked the buzz they gave my head. At that time, I chose to smoke and built a 2 pack-a-day habit for 22 years. I enjoyed the experience until at the age of 38 I began to notice the burn holes in my clothes, the cigarette droppings at the table, my shortness of breath, and a morning cough. For these and more reasons, several years ago, I finally was able, after five unsuccessful attempts, to put them aside. Multidimensional excuses, personal views of myself and my world, plus my attitudes had to be confronted before I could accomplish my liberation from this habit. Cigarettes had become an integral part of my relationship to myself and to the world around me.

I had to look at what I was gaining, what was my payoff, the emotions involved, and the history I had with my initial decision to take up this habit. I had to rethink each previous decision that had created my dependency on nicotine. With journal work, I discovered I didn't feel I deserved to take a break from work unless I called it a "cig break". In tense situations, I thought I needed a cigarette to calm my thoughts. The former decision had to do with my self-image, the second had to do with smoke-screening my feelings. These were views of myself I had created by choice.

Thus, I challenged myself to create a new self-image by making new decisions. It wasn't just an intellectual exercise. It was filled with fear, anxiety, sadness, and anger. Each emotional experience was supported with my REIKI hands and with each new decision, I was able to rebuild a "me" who could make the "change of mind" necessary to live without smoking.

I also have to accept the fact that twenty-two years of smoking has left me with a decreased ability to breathe on exertion. My teeth are brittle from the years of hot fumes passing over them.

I'm not attempting, here, to lecture on the evils of smoking. I am using my experience simply to illustrate how my decisions affected my life and breath and led me to experiences I did not like and brought me into a situation which is still greatly affecting the quality of my life.

Ultimately, all decisions direct our lives as to whether or not we are going to get sick with certain diseases, and to a degree, whether we are going to place ourselves in positions that could lead to accidents, or be in environments where catastrophes can happen.

It is very difficult to accept that our choices are responsible for whatever happens to our body. No one wants to believe that he or she might have chosen their car accident or their cancer, or be responsible in any way for any upsetting incident in their life. In fact, the realization of this responsibility is invariably painful. But it is this very understanding that can help to explain the intricacies of the healing process.

Whatever our background or experience in health or in healing, it's important to begin to understand this complexity. Just as one decision builds on another to create disharmony, disease, etc, we can build a new set of choices which will determine to what degree we have chosen to be healed.

Takata's advice was to do regular and consistent REIKI sessions for a chronically ill patient. Consecutive REIKI sessions give the body, mind, emotions, and the spirit a chance to come together in a relaxed and energize state. A chance, as it were, to rethink individual and collective decisions on some (or every) level. An opportunity, in the quiet, to sort through past selections and experiences. All of this can occur without the practitioner or the client being aware that it's happening.

I believe that what we see as "miraculous healings" are actually the coming together of this energy, REIKI, which facilitates the rebalancing of a total being, and any individual who has decided on all levels to accept and hold onto that balance. For some persons, this moment can be instantaneous, and a miracle is announced. We hear and read of these frequently. For most of us, the degree of rebalancing comes steadily or in small increments, and this is what we see in ourselves and in our REIKI practices.

On some occasions, we will see a transformation during one session, but then a gradual return to the original problem. The body might have been willing, but the emotions or thoughts or attitudes were not ready for the change.

Just as it is with any decision to create a new experience, we cannot know what the experience is until we make the decision to do it. Any movement from one habit or view of life to another cannot be known to its fullest extent until we decide to do it and accomplish it.

To continue with my personal example, I could not have realized that setting tobacco aside would change the pattern of my marriage relationship or open up a new challenge of self-discovery around co-dependency. I had no idea that it would increase my dislike for certain odors. I decided to return to smoking several times until I had made decisions as to how to deal with these and other challenges. My REIKI hands on my body's areas of tension helped me remain calm enough to work through these situations.

Thus, REIKI helps us recognize our opportunities to make any choice or decision we wish.

Remember always, just as this decision to

create disease is personal, so is the decision to create health. Each person will do it in their own way. Some of us may decided as we are expected to. Others of us may make the ultimate healing decision to let loose of this life experience.

Keep in mind then that as practitioners or for ourselves, we are only present to facilitate the decision-making process by channeling REIKI and being present without judgement.

Space and Permission

Have you ever noticed how individuals take their places in waiting areas or classrooms where there are plenty of seats? Commonly a person will sit with an empty seat on either side. If the entire room becomes crowded, most people will keep their places. At other times, if the vacant seats are filled, some individuals will leave.

Have you ever watched two people in conversation? One leans forward to emphasize a point and the other backs away. When the first returns to their original stance, the second one returns also. In effect, a consistent yardage has been maintained between their bodies.

When I began to notice this happening to me, I initially worried about body odor or possible bad breath. Then, in a communications seminar, I became aware of this concept of personal space.

Theories and descriptions vary in their interpretation. Some authorities believe there is an area around the body that is charged by the presence of an etheric body created by our unique electromagnetic fields. Others feel it is a manifestation of various degrees of energy which can be seen as auras of color and intensity. Another group thinks it may be heat emanations from the metabolism of our cells.

Whatever the explanation, there is one thing that can be agreed upon. Every individual on this planet has a comfort zone around their body. Not only does personal space have cultural, family training, and situational factors, it also has a relationship to the quality and quantity of sleep obtained the night before, what's been eaten, and what feelings are held about personal physique as well as an individual's state of emotional, mental, and spiritual being.

The width of these spaces has been documented by thermal sensitive machines and energy detectors. Sensitive people have been known to train themselves to feel these 'spaces' around others' bodies. Changes in these fields have been noted and it has been discovered that arguments tend to increase the need for depth and width of personal space. The decision to be intimate decreases or thins it.

Communication studies claim that interpersonal relationships can be enhanced when attention is paid to individual comfort zones.

My further study of this manifestation, especially with mild to moderately ill patients has increased my awareness of just how intrusive, or how welcome, "touch" becomes in the healing process.

Time and sensitivity is needed to understand the relevancy of another person's ability to be touched. Just having a patient or a client make an appointment is not carte blanche permission to place our hands on their body.

I like the Usui System of Natural Healing, even more now because I realize it is one of the least threatening bodywork techniques. It does not require the client to become naked and exposed. Layers of blankets can be used if an individual so desires. REIKI goes through them.

REIKI also is employed in a pattern that does not overwhelmingly invade an individual's comfort zone. When the first head position is utilized as the first touch position in a session, oftentimes it is the best, least invasive of all touches.

Remember the traditionally dramatized comfort of a mother's touch? Most often it is a stroke across the brow of her child. An initial lover's touch usually involves a hand upon a face. A kiss on the forehead can be the first contact of intimacy. REIKI is employed in a similar approach.

Starting a session at the head and over the eyes and brow begins relaxation of the mental body and softens thoughts, perceptions, and personal issues. This 'beginning' reduces anxiety and invites relaxation, the primary need of an over-stressed body. I like to call this "putting the mind at ease".

Even though a client may relax initially, it is important to allow for any change of comfort zone while on the table. At any time during a session, a personal alarm system may go off, announcing that some wall or barrier has been breached. This can be recognized by discomfort on a client's face, or twitching that is not like the twitching of sleep, but more like a restlessness. This may signal a disturbance and needs to be addressed by encouraging any client to feel in charge of the session.

Allow them to adjust to their level of comfort and briefly express, if possible, their distress. This encourages them to relax their guard and allows for increased absorption of REIKI. It also involves them in a special way by assisting them to maintain a sense of self. This involvement does not mean they may chatter constantly about their day or their family or their job. This means they can express their discomfort in sound, breath, or words.

Obtaining permission at the beginning of any session may be formal or informal. Become aware of any clues an individual may give you regarding their hesitancy to get on the table face up or to begin a session that is foreign to their experience.

If reluctance is present, we can offer to place our hands on an area that is causing them discomfort and illustrate the sensation of warmth or vibration that underneath when placed on an area of need. If, after this demonstration, they still seem uncomfortable, question them about their reason for coming or suggest that another time may be better.

The more acknowledgement we give our client's right to their body and their space, the more often we will be given permission to touch and offer REIKI for their benefit.

After the Emergency

We CAN use REIKI in emergency situations to staunch the flow of blood, to retard the destruction of tissue from a burn, and to keep swelling to a minimum. We can offer our hands to those in an acute respiratory crisis, to assist in the reduction of pain, or to calm anxiety until medical assistance arrives.

Application of REIKI can be focused on all acute symptoms except a broken bone until it is set in place. After any emergency, to promote health and balance to the entire system that has been traumatized, a total body session is suggested.

Our arms and legs are not independent appendages of our hearts or lungs. Every component of our cardiac, circulatory, respiratory, lymphatic, enzymatic, etc., systems are tied into each other and when one part becomes injured, this entire complex does not just go on standby, it goes into action.

The energy depletion of our body's systems and the toxic waste that is produced after it has been on emergency duty can create further damage to its intricate balance.

Sometimes it is not convenient to stand by the side of a hospital bed for a structured session. Sometimes all that can be managed is a reassuring touch and calm word. This is where REIKI's ability to be transferred from cell to cell assists us. We can hold a hand or a foot and know that, in a space of time, the entire body will receive the energy boost it needs to accomplish its healing.

If time is available, it is always wise to follow-up an emergency problem with a full session. If it's not possible, what you have done is put to use, in the best way possible, what you have at hand.

Intuition

Recently I was asked if there is another way in which to perform the Usui System. This individual had been working with REIKI for many years and, whereas he accepted the value of doing the total session of precise hand positions, he felt he had been drawn to touch other areas that had not been covered in the formalized session.

I have two reactions. Both are supported by personal observations.

The first relies heavily on Takata's teachings that dictate:

"Put the major organs in balance and energize them, and healing will happen."

This is a good practice because oftentimes, when a client comes with a specific ailment or symptom, the entire body is out of balance.

In my experience, accomplishing the entire hands-on session will reduce or eliminate the specific complaint at the end.

There are times when I will add positions after having completed the head and front sections. My decision to do so is based on my second reaction regarding how to do a full-body session.

I have observed that my hands, simply speaking, take over.

If I can accept the fact that REIKI is pulled through my body in a degree proportionate to the need that is under my hand and I can test that out time and time again on myself and others, then I can come to accept the fact that this energy responds to need.

When my hands are in the air as I'm talking, I do not usually have a sensation of pulsation or vibration or heat or coolness. If I place my hand on the telephone receiver or the table or some other object that does not have an identifiable hurt or imbalance, my hand remains "my hand'.

It's when I get around a plant or animal or human being who has an ache or a stress or strain, and I place my hand there, it becomes something more. It has a different feel to it. I perceive it as becoming fuller, or itching, or vi-brating, etc.

After many years of this, I've realized that my hands are drawn to a specific place or pain or stress. It's as if the potential energy through my hands is searching for a way to express itself, searching out a need to fill.

How many times have many of us heard, "How did you know I hurt there?" or "My goodness, I didn't know I was so tense until you touched me!"

I repeat, it is not as if I consciously decided to place my hand on a particular spot. My hand was moved there and a connection was made. I am becoming convinced that this is a by-product of the non-judgmental, non-expectation-oriented practice of REIKI. A level of intuition is developed that goes beyond what the mind perceives.

It is this occurrence, I believe, that may also move this system away from a practice that is easily documentable. It could very well be the reason that some health providers and practitioners won't authenticate REIKI. When they ask, "How does it work?" or "Why did you do that?"; the answer comes, "I'm not sure," or "I don't know," or "I just do it and it works."

My only suggestion is one of caution. If when you are doing the structured approach, you "feel" your hands being drawn to a different position on your client's body, do so. You'll know if there is a need there by the way your hands react. Then move on to the next structured hand position, or move with the sense of your hands. It is best to be certain all the usual positions are covered by the end of the session.

You will then be able to document for yourself the wonder of "following the intuition" of your hands and still accomplish the dictates of Takata.

THE FINAL QUESTION

To see you pale and hairless
    In pain, with tiny pupils
To hear your whispered voice ask
        no longer, "Why?" but "When?"
    I feel the pressure build
      behind my eyes
          And around my heart.

To sit and breathe with you,
To wonder indeed which breath
      Will be your last,
    I feel my throat tighten with
        a flood of unspoken words
        and of unshed tears.

To know there may not be
      Many tomorrows.
That all there is
      May be this moment
        Of watching with you
        Of waiting with you
      For the start of your
        Next adventure
I find myself holding my breath
      Then sighing a prayer
        That your question
          Will soon be answered.

For Sue, 1989
Excerpted from "Attitudes of Dying"

Hospice

Sometimes the ultimate healing decision is to let loose of this life experience. This occurrence for any practitioner of any healing modality or medical providership challenges the very existence of our practice and beliefs.

All too often, we can get ourselves into an over-focused attitude of wanting each of our clients to attain health in a way that embraces life as we know it.

It comes as a shock to accomplish a REIKI session and feel as if our hands have merely moved from one position to another. We may have brought some kind of comfort, but the energy has not passed to the places we have touched.

Even more uncomfortably, I have been in a position where my touch brought increased pain.

The heat from my hand caused such discomfort that the person I was working on was reduced to tears. In one case, I couldn't bring my hand any closer to her body than two feet.

I was so distressed at this I had to leave the room. Why, after all these years when I had been able to ease anxiety and discomfort, stop bleeding, unknot muscle spasms, did my hand bring discomfort to the closest friend I had when she needed relief from her cancerous pain? I haven't come to the bottom-line answer yet, but I do have sense of what was happening.

When, on a personal level, an individual makes the decision to embrace the other side of life, in most cases, the need for REIKI, Universal Life Energy, no longer exists. The cells and tissues of the body have no need to be energized. They are relinquishing their duties, so to speak, as are all the functions of the body, and they are shutting down. It is the way that death of the body occurs.

Even if the person is saying that they want to live, somehow, on some level, a decision has been made to pass on to whatever they believe is next. Sometimes, when following the hands-on technique, parts of the body will continue to accept energy and other parts will not.

This, of course, isn't a hard and fast rule. There are, in the course of a session, many times when an individual has so much armoring in a

80

particular place, there is a block to the draw of energy from my hands. Sometimes these areas eventually accept REIKI during the session. Individuals who are experiencing a life-threatening illness and who have this armoring, I have discovered, open only minimally to this energy and then only to areas of emotional pain and mental anguish which are around the heart, front and back, and on all head positions. I believe that this is a sign that a client is making peace with themselves and reaching for the ultimate healing.

Working with hospice patients who have all kinds of illnesses is an experience not just in dealing with death and dying, but in dealing with life. Our personal values can be challenged and our understanding of the quality of life can be enhanced. REIKI is always there to help.

In one reported case in the AIDS Outreach Program, a young man was living in an isolation room on a hospital ward in Seattle, Washington. He was considered obnoxious, demanding and complaining and few nurses would 'gown up' to enter his room even though they knew he was fearful and anxious.

A friend recommended REIKI Outreach but he initially rejected the session. The REIKI volunteer persevered, however, put on the required gown, hat, shoes, and gloves, and performed the total body session in his hospital room.

With just one session, the young man was able to release a large percentage of his hostility and aggression and became less anxious. Perhaps it was the fact that someone voluntarily took the time to be in his room and to touch him in a non-judgmental fashion. Perhaps it was also the fact that his need for attention was met by the transference of REIKI. In any event, it is reported that with each REIKI session he changed.

Before he passed on, he was able to relate in a much more rewarding manner for himself and the nurses and doctors. His was a room that always had someone stopping in even if they had to go through the process of gowning and un-gowning. REIKI helped him change and to pass on with less fear and anxiety.

For those experiencing chemotherapy, REIKI can reduce the side effects so therapy can be tolerated to a greater degree. When radiation is prescribed, REIKI assists surrounding tissues to resist breakdown. Post-surgical healing is enhanced with REIKI. Anxiety is reduced so communication regarding difficult personal subjects can be accomplished.

REIKI is a very supportive method for family members during terminal care of their loved ones. REIKI is also very beneficial to Hospice Volunteers. REIKI could have helped those nurses in Seattle ease their anxieties too.

My most recent occasion of Hospice work saw me attending to the last days of a terminally-ill patient who happened to be a very dear friend. She spoke of her desire to move on to her next adventure and asked continually how she could let go of this life.

My hands would become warm when I entered her room, and caused her too much discomfort when I touched her. I learned that as I sat by her bedside, my hands were best placed on my chest or heart. I was able to calm myself so I could be there for her in the best way I knew how. I could take care of my pain of losing her and still be present. Feeling the warmth of my own hand on my chest kept me centered and helped me to cry when it was the most appropriate and to continue helping her and others who came to assist or visit her.

Working with patients who are dying is not for everyone. Experiencing death in others is something that will occur to each of us. However we are called upon to serve with REIKI, our hands are always with us and will attend to whatever is the need.

Alternative vs. Complementary

We've come a long way from the horse and buggy days of medicine, when the black bag-carrying doctor knew his patients from birth to death as well as their previous family history. New findings and research results are being announced weekly. New diagnostic tools are created yearly. In order for a doctor to know as much as possible about any segment of medicine, he/she is almost required to specialize.

Unfortunately, because we are also a mobile society, many doctors are even farther removed from having a past history available on each of his patients. To study and treat symptoms only is then an outgrowth of medical specialization and societal transience.

When the concept of viewing each patient as a totality reappeared and became established under the title of Holistic (or Wholistic) Medicine,

85

there was hope that people could find a medical provider who would address an illness with attention to an individual's myriad inter-relationships.

Now there is a full field of Holistic practitioners. There are Iridologists, Reflexologists, Colonic Therapists, Rebirthers, Energy Workers, Massage Therapists, Jin Shin Do Therapists, Hypnotherapists, Color or Art and Music Therapists. The list goes on and on with all kinds of methods and manners of healing work.

What has developed over the years is another group of specialists, designated as Alternative Therapies or Alternative Medicine.

Somehow, looking at the total patient has become divided and specialized again and according to the definition of the word, alternative, we have become "the other choice."

Allopathic and Holistic Medicine can work together. I can speak from experience.

Over a period of four years, I tried several types of "alternative" therapies to reduce my uterine fibroids. I took Vitamin A therapy, was on a vegetarian diet, used visualization, did counseling and hypnotherapy, worked with crystals, attended American Indian Healing Ceremonies, and constantly performed REIKI on myself. The fibroids reduced then returned. I then reviewed issues regarding my femaleness, guilt, shame, anger, and frustration. The fibroids diminished and then returned again. I was at the end of my rope.

At the urging of a fellow nurse, I came to realize that I had done a lot of healing work on myself but that I wasn't yet a magician. I needed help to remove the growths, so I went to a Gynecologist and had a hysterectomy and was then able to use all the skills I had learned to return to an improved level of energy and activity. I needed that operation and I needed all the techniques I had learned to obtain the healing I desired. I came together as the person I am today because I combined therapies, and I know they can come together for others.

Holistic Medicine, then, in my present understanding, can stand for both Allopathic and Alternative Methods. It is an attitudinal approach to health care because it treats each case of accident or disease as a total experience of the individual.

X-ray can be combined with Hypnotherapeutic Counseling. Pain-control medicine can be enhanced with hands-on energy transfer. Chemotherapy then can be potentiated by Guided Imagery. Surgery and muscle rehabilitation can be improved with Physical and Music Therapy. All the methods can co-operate. They can complement each other.

Look at Webster's definition of Complementary:

> "That which completes or makes perfect.....the quantity or amount which when added completes a whole; either of two parts or things needed to complete each other."

Perhaps we can work toward redefining all procedures, therapies, and health support systems under the title of Complementary Therapies so that each individual can have a grand scope of possibilities available for his/her decision-making process regarding health and healing.

That truly would be Total Health Care, or TLC (Total Life Care).

Responsible REIKI

I became especially concerned recently when I heard of a REIKI practitioner who told a client, "Don't go to see your doctor for two weeks while we're doing REIKI." This request was made of a woman who had been diagnosed as having an ovarian cyst that was possibly malignant. A two week delay can be life-threatening in ovarian cancer and this kind of request, whether or not the cyst disappears, places the client, the practitioner, and REIKI in jeopardy.

In another recent case, a man with glaucoma was told that one session with REIKI could cure his condition. Whether or not this occurs, the statement alone puts all involved in a potentially hazardous position.

We can have no idea how or what any body will become as we nurture it.

For example, when I was working in ICU, I cared for a teenage girl who had fallen from a horse onto a pitchfork which had penetrated her brain and left her paralyzed and comatose. At the head of her bed were pictures of what she had been; long hair, bright eyes, wide-open smile. I know they were placed there to give us nurses in ICU an opportunity to focus on who she was as a person rather than the unresponsive body on the bed, attached to the respirator.

I also know the trick it played on all our minds. After three months the young girl rolled out of the hospital in her wheelchair still partially paralyzed with slurred speech. Our ICU Head Nurse came back from the girl's send-off in tears because she couldn't help but compare the youngster, at the time of discharge, to the active, capable young person she had appeared to be in the pictures before the accident.

Healing had occurred but she had survived in a different form than hoped for, leaving us with a sense of failure.

It is also true that whenever I try to picture a friend or a patient/client well or whole, my mind moves most often to a picture that is previous to the present.

The pictures of the young girl as well as those I've held in my mind of a sick friend limits the possibilities and sets a case for disappointment.

90

So does any element of expectation in "making someone whole." We cannot know what that wholeness is. The person we are working with rarely has a clear understanding for their own personal wholeness.

I am not saying that hope is to be denied, only that we must take care in all areas of health treatment and support therapies to relinquish any expectation of a specific result.

We can be ready for change. We cannot predict what that change will be. We also may not dictate what that change must be for anyone.

It is true that miraculous changes have been recorded with the use of REIKI. However, it is the setting up for the expectation of those changes that is most often a need of the practitioner to plan or control the outcome. This is inappropriate and detrimental to the practice of REIKI and predisposes us to failure as an acceptable part of the team for health and health care in the United States.

We must use our system with care and responsibility. We must forego the temptation to "make things right," to place our egos on the line and to pretend we know what the outcome of any REIKI session may be.

I have come to the place now, that all I promise is that something will change, or that a change will occur. I leave it up to the individual to be sensitive to his/her body so as to be aware of whatever that change is. I only promise that for REIKI to work, it has to be used. I am taking the guesswork out of the results of a session, because I make no guesses.

Note also that I say "session". In my mind, at this time, because we are not legally allowed to treat anyone, I have changed my approach to stating that I have REIKI sessions, or hands-on sessions. I also have a Disclaimer for signing at each session. **I encourage individuals to see their doctor on a regular basis, to continue to have their condition and health monitored, and never to stop taking any medication unless they check with their doctor first.**

When changes occur in people who come to me for sessions, I ask if they would be willing to help me document those changes. This can ultimately assist the Usui System of Natural Healing to collect accurate and thorough observations for the medical community.

I believe that I am not only protecting myself, I believe I am protecting REIKI by not putting it out on a limb. REIKI is too important to allow it to become challenged unnecessarily.

MANTRA

My soul cries for enough space

        within which to roam

   But also enough limits

        by which to be guided.

My soul prays for enough silence

        within which to find peace,

   But also enough words

        by which to express itself.

My soul seeks enough aloneness

        in which to develop

   And enough touching

        by which to announce its

        Presence.

For the Future

Did you know that REIKI is being taught in Virginia as Healing Hands and that the Radiance Technique, as well as Radiant REIKI, Mari-El and the Teachings of the Cauldron of Thoth have their origins in the Usui System of Natural Healing? There is now also an "Usui Lightworks" as well as a Master's Symbol fashioned out of magnetized metal and plastic, and a reworked version of our teachings named Omega.

Another REIKI group offers First and Second Degree Classes on the same weekend, and a third organization initiates interested students to all three levels over three days. There is a system that has 'seven degrees' of REIKI.

There are as many variations and interpretations of REIKI being taught now as there are individuals to teach. This has brought conflict, anger, and jealousy.

These reactions create confusion and doubt in the minds of other bodyworkers and medical professionals as to any documentable cause and effect of REIKI. The various changes and our various reactions also undermine our credibility.

I find I'm frustrated by these changes and reactions. How can REIKI become validated enough to be addressed with any kind of seriousness by the medical profession so that we can somehow begin to work together?

The only way I can begin to understand why there are so many methods is to return to my own experience.

When I first began practicing the Usui System, I felt I was on the crest of a wave. My perceptions were heightened. I was personally convinced that REIKI was the answer to the ills of mankind and womankind. I still believe this but in the context that any connection with Universal Life Energy, however a person wants to name it and in whatever form or system he or she wants to practice it, can be transformational.

Through the Usui System, I feel I experienced an opening of my inner voice and developed an increased capacity to hear. My mind and hands were guided to places on a person's body. I sensed messages regarding the sensations in my hands. I heard voices which urged me to say certain things to my clients or to have them picture certain colors under my hands. I received ideas about how to assist a client to look into a past life or lives for information regarding their infirmities.

I also began reading more about Color Therapy, Light Therapy, and Hypnosis. I had already taken classes in Aura Reading, Guided Imagery, Peer-Crisis Counseling, Chakra Balancing. I began to sense myself in a kind of frenzy, to do all, to be all, encompass all. I saw everything as it seemed to fit together but I couldn't **bring** it all together.

I had also added so much to my practice of REIKI, I had overlaid the basic gift of balance and re-energizing by adding other methods and techniques. Because REIKI is so simple, I had decided that REIKI needed to be more and I had made it so complicated that my clients had become more dependent on me, not less.

When I brought my heightened perceptions and visions to my clients, they were grateful for the information, but in the end, I felt much as Usui must have felt in his story with the beggars in the slums of Tokyo. The changes I had expected and envisioned in these clients were not forthcoming. They were my expectations and visions, not theirs. I was in essence telling them their process rather than allowing them to live it on their own.

This is what I believe is happening in the vast arena of New Age developments and with REIKI.

Each individual has had an awakening to the energy, to the light, to what is beyond this earth plane. Because we are each unique prisms of light from the Creator, of the Goddess Mother, or the Great Spirit, or Buddha (whichever system of belief you subscribe to...) we each have our set of perspectives on this life and our individually designed set of skills and gifts. The awakening that happens for each of us when we are ready to allow it to occur brings us into contact with all the possibilities and, most importantly, our individual uniqueness. The energy, being universal, touches those gifts and makes them part of our growth as well as part of the way we express ourselves to the world in which we relate.

The many different classes and methods that have been developed are being created in response to the instructor's individual awakening. He or she is offering **their** awareness and self-discovery as a new method. It works for them; it can work for everyone.

It is here that a big problem occurs, as I see it. A bit of ego gets in the way. The self-discovery no longer becomes "my way"; it becomes "The Way", leading directly to competition and separation, which in turn creates conflict, anger, and jealousies.

In my opinion, no two persons can really share, "The Way". It becomes instead a matter of a teacher or a guru or a Master teaching their personal discovery which removes from students their responsibility to experience their own awakening as well as their own truths through their own unique skills and gifts.

We each have our own lessons.

Thus, I only teach the Usui System of Natural Healing, and I teach it as closely as possible to the traditional mode. I use tapes of Takata speaking and teaching to keep me on track. I want to leave each student open to his or her own growth pattern. REIKI is a new beginning, not the middle, and never the end. It adds and expands each of our worlds so that we each may be healthier and more able to stand as unique individuals.

To grapple with the fact that there are so many REIKI methods out there, I have begun to understand that all of them are natural outgrowths of a successful system.

We are not the only system that has been or is being changed by personal vision or "divine" guidance. History shows how religions have splintered and new denominations have developed. Medical Science continues to split itself apart when a new specialty is developed and recognized. In the Holistic Arena, there is a new kind of energy therapy or bodywork movement being designed constantly.

Our challenge will be the standard of integrity

which each of us brings to our art, therapeutic skill, or method, practice or session. We will also be challenged to live in peace with the many approaches that have developed regarding how to transfer REIKI or any other named form of energy. We will be confronted with the possibility of creating some kind of underlying consensus of technique so that REIKI can be documented.

Because we are truly on the verge of changing our world, we need as many enlightened and loving people as can emerge. We need as many methods as there are individuals so that something will speak to everyone.

Helping each other along the way is the process by which we help ourselves. Especially if we can help each other without judgement and with respect for our individual processes. This, in itself, can establish an ethical guide of practice and purpose.

The continuation of life on this planet in a healthy way and within a healthy environment requires our attitudes encompass all possibilities and that we monitor ourselves responsibly, while continuing to offer ourselves and our gifts to all.

The Challenge

There are many methods by which to channel energy. The Usui System of Natural Healing is but one. There are many ways of saying energy. REIKI is the name I use, along with thousands of others.

You may wish to learn another method or incorporate many techniques to create your own unique style. Whatever you are guided to do, please know, that at this time, you have allowed yourself the gift of healing energy and it is in your hands.

It's simple. It is also enough.

It's now up to you......

REIKI

WILL ONLY WORK

IF

YOU USE IT!

ABOUT THE AUTHOR:

Earlene Gleisner continues to live with her husband and to work as a Registered Nurse and Health Educator in a small rural community in Northern California. She travels to wherever there are interested students, providing CE credit for RNs, and maintains a private REIKI practice.

"REIKI For Professionals" will be available in early 1994. Descriptions and suggestions of how any skilled worker (mother to machinist, clergyman to teacher, or doctor to dog catcher) can use REIKI in their work will be presented. One essay shows how REIKI stands alone in the world of multiple therapies through its simple application; another compares REIKI with Therapeutic Touch. This second book of stories and essays is offered to those who wish to extend themselves to the rest of the world as REIKI practitioners and to those in the rest of the world who may wish to understand a little more about REIKI.

"Attitudes of Dying", a handbook for Hospice Volunteers, "Changing By Choice", a workbook for Tobacco Cessation, and "That's The Spirit!" as well as two fictional novels, "Second Chances" and "The Bundle" are in process.

All correspondence will be answered.

To order:

REIKI IN EVERYDAY LIVING (#)_____

To order/reserve:

REIKI FOR PROFESSIONALS (#)_____

@ 12.95   EQUALS   _____
CA Tax (.0725)   _____
SHIPPING (2.00 first   _____
    and .50 additional)
TOTAL (enclosed)   _____
                          (US DOLLARS)

(Discounts available to REIKI Masters   a n d
book stores. Wiring instructions for overseas
orders on dealer or Master discount flyers.)

Checks Payable to:
WHITE FEATHER PRESS
POB 1209, Laytonville, CA 95454
(707)984-6048